FUN FACT FILE: FOUNDING FATHERS

20 FUN FACTS ABOUT JAMES MADISON

By Arthur K. Britton

Gareth Stevens
PUBLISHING

Please visit our website, www.garethstevens.com. For a free color catalog of all our high-quality books, call toll free 1-800-542-2595 or fax 1-877-542-2596.

Library of Congress Cataloging-in-Publication Data
Names: Britton, Arthur K., author.
Title: 20 fun facts about James Madison / Arthur K. Britton.
Other titles: Twenty fun facts about James Madison
Description: New York : Gareth Stevens Publishing, [2018] | Series: Fun fact
  file: founding fathers | Includes index.
Identifiers: LCCN 2017000905| ISBN 9781538202913 (pbk. book) | ISBN
  9781538202739 (6 pack) | ISBN 9781538202852 (library bound book)
Subjects: LCSH: Madison, James, 1751-1836–Juvenile literature. |
  Presidents–United States–Biography–Juvenile literature. |
  Statesmen–United States–Biography–Juvenile literature.
Classification: LCC E342 .B75 2018 | DDC 973.51092092 [B] –dc23
LC record available at https://lccn.loc.gov/2017000905

First Edition

Published in 2018 by
Gareth Stevens Publishing
111 East 14th Street, Suite 349
New York, NY 10003

Copyright © 2018 Gareth Stevens Publishing

Designer: Sam DeMartin
Editor: Ryan Nagelhout

Photo credits: Cover, p. 1 (background) Fine Art Images/Getty Images; cover, pp. 1 (portrait), 18 Everett-Art/Shutterstock.com; pp. 5, 22 Everett Historical/Shutterstock.com; p. 6 Danita Delimont/Getty Images; p. 7 Djkeddie/Wikimedia Commons; p. 8 Fœ/Wikimedia Commons; pp. 9, 14, 29 DEA PICTURE LIBRARY/Getty Images; p. 10 Ritu Manoj Jethani/Shutterstock.com; p. 11 Bettmann/Bettmann/Getty Images; p. 12 Pi.1415926535/Wikimedia Commons; p. 13 courtesy of the Library of Congress; p. 15 Jarodalien/ Wikimedia Commons; p. 16 (background) Larrybob/Wikimedia Commons; p. 16 (portrait) Jonund/Wikimedia Commons; pp. 17, 24 UniversalImagesGroup/Universal Images Group/Getty Images; p. 19 Dawn Hudson/ Shutterstock.com; p. 20 Jose Gil/Shutterstock.com; p. 21 Hutsuliak Dmytro/Shutterstock.com; p. 23 Eric Isselee/Shutterstock.com; p. 25 Billy Hathorn/Wikimedia Commons; p. 26 Glow Images, Inc/Getty Images.

Printed in China

CPSIA compliance information: Batch #CS17GS: For further information contact Gareth Stevens, New York, New York at 1-800-542-2595.

Contents

Words in the glossary appear in **bold** type the first time they are used in the text.

Man of Many Titles

James Madison had a list of titles as long as your arm! He was one of America's Founding Fathers. He's been called the Father of the **Constitution** for his important part in shaping it.

As a member of the newly formed US House of **Representatives**, he was Congressman Madison. He served as President Thomas Jefferson's secretary of state. And then he became President Madison. But there's much more to Madison than these titles. Keep reading to uncover some unusual and wonderful facts about our fourth president!

Madison was named after his father, so his full name was James Madison Jr. He was born March 16, 1751, and died June 28, 1836.

Young Madison

FACT 1

Madison was the oldest of a dozen, or 12, children!

Maybe his parents thought they were really cheaper by the dozen. With that many children around, it's almost like a party all the time! The children grew up on the family plantation, or large farm, in Orange County, Virginia.

Madison's family plantation was named Montpelier (mahnt-PIHL-yuhr).

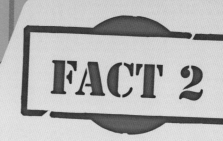

FACT 2

Madison's horse helped him get an education.

In 1769, Madison left Montpelier to attend the **College** of

New Jersey—riding from Virginia to

New Jersey on his horse! He was

such a bright, hardworking

student that he completed all

his studies in 2 years instead

of the usual 4 years. His

health, however, suffered.

This picture of Madison was made while he was a student at the College of New Jersey. The college is now known as Princeton University.

FACT 3

Madison had some killer friends.

One of Madison's friends at college was Aaron Burr. Burr fought in the American Revolution, the colonies' war for independence from England. He served as Thomas Jefferson's vice president. But he's most famous for killing Alexander Hamilton, another Founding Father, in a **duel**!

This is an artist's idea of what the duel between Burr and Hamilton was like at the moment Burr shot Hamilton.

No one ever said Madison was a man who "stood tall."

Madison was a small, sickly child. As a grown man, he was only 5 feet 4 inches (163 cm) tall and weighed only about 100 pounds (45 kg). He was the shortest president in US history!

Madison was also said to have a weak voice.

FACT 5

During the American Revolution, Madison fought with words instead of guns.

Madison's poor health prevented him from serving in the military during the war. Instead, he entered **politics** to serve the young nation taking shape. In 1776—the year the colonies announced their freedom from England—he helped Virginia form a new, independent state government.

This is the Capitol Building in Williamsburg, Virginia, where Madison began his political life.

Madison met his BFF while working in Virginia's new state government.

Madison met and became friends with Thomas Jefferson during his work in Virginia's government. Their friendship lasted for life. It was because of their friendship that Madison became Jefferson's secretary of state in 1801. He served until 1809.

Here, Madison and his friend Jefferson talk about the location of the young nation's future capital.

Madison was so shy he spent 6 months at the Second Continental Congress before he said anything.

Madison was picked to attend the Second Continental Congress when it met in Philadelphia, Pennsylvania, in March 1780. He was the youngest delegate, or representative, there. When he finally decided to speak, he spoke so well that he quickly became a leader in the congress.

The Second Continental Congress is shown here voting on independence.

FACT 8

Madison wrote letters using secret codes!

Madison worried the wrong person might get hold of one of his letters that included important private political facts. So he wrote using secret codes. Madison wasn't the only political leader to do this. Jefferson and others did so as well.

Despite his big role, Madison didn't think he should be called the Father of the Constitution. He said it was "the work of many heads and many hands."

FACT 9

You could say Madison was Mother as well as Father of the Constitution.

Without Madison, the Constitution wouldn't have been born. He set the wheels in motion that led to the **Constitutional Convention**. Madison wrote the Virginia Plan, which supplied the basic frame for the Constitution. He also wrote newspaper articles that helped get the Constitution **ratified**.

Madison was one of the best notetakers in history.

How do we know what happened at the Constitutional Convention so many years ago? How do we know who said what? Madison took careful, exact day-by-day notes, which supply the only complete history we have of the convention!

These are some notes Madison made for a speech about amendments, or changes, to the Constitution in 1789.

FACT 11

Madison immediately became part of the new government he helped create.

Madison was elected to the newly formed US House of Representatives in 1789. One of the first things he did was write the Bill of Rights. That's the first 10 amendments, or changes, to the Constitution that list the basic rights held by US citizens.

Madison once suggested renting Portugal's navy.

While Madison was in Congress, the United States was seeking a way to keep its trading ships safe. One way would be for the country to build a navy. Instead, Madison suggested renting the navy of the European nation of Portugal!

Pirates, or robbers, from northern Africa captured US trading ships and demanded money to set them free. President Jefferson sent ships to fight the pirates in 1801.

We can thank Madison, along with Thomas Jefferson, for creating America's two-party political system.

As a congressman, Madison opposed ideas of Alexander Hamilton, leader of the Federalist Party. Madison and Jefferson supported states' rights and objected to Hamilton's idea of a national bank. So they founded the Democratic-Republican Party, and the two-party system was born.

Jefferson, Madison, and James Monroe, shown here, were the only Democratic-Republicans ever to become president. The party broke apart in the 1820s.

WISE WORDS FROM MADISON

"If men were angels, no government would be necessary."

"A people who mean to be their own governors must arm themselves with the power which knowledge gives."

"The man who is possessed of wealth . . . cannot judge the wants or feelings of the day-laborer."

"The accumulation [gathering] of all powers . . . in the same hands . . . may justly be pronounced the very definition of tyranny."

FACT 14

Madison captured Spanish West Florida in a secret war.

Without telling Congress, Madison used soldiers to capture West Florida from Spain. He claimed it as part of the Louisiana Territory, which the United States had purchased from France in 1803.

UNITED STATES

West Florida

What was called West Florida didn't include any of modern Florida. It covered parts of the present-day states of Alabama, Mississippi, and Louisiana.

Madison's hobbies included reading ancient Greek and Latin books—in their original languages.

Founding Fathers such as George Washington and Jefferson had many hobbies, including farming and creating plans for new buildings. Madison had few, and though his hobbies might not sound like much fun to you, he enjoyed them!

Madison also enjoyed playing chess. Chess is a game for two players that requires thinking ahead, planning, and skill.

FACT 16

Madison loved ice cream.

In Madison's day, ice cream was a treat indeed. You couldn't simply go to the store to buy ice cream. It took a great deal of hard work to make it. Madison and his wife, Dolley, both loved ice cream and often served it at official White House events.

Dolley Madison's favorite ice cream flavor was oyster!

The White House pet when Madison was president was a green parrot.

Many presidents have had pets. Mostly, they've been dogs. But there have also been cats, hamsters, rabbits, ponies, parakeets, and horses. The green parrot in Madison's White House actually belonged to Dolley.

Perhaps Dolley Madison's green parrot looked something like this.

For his **inauguration**, Madison wore clothes made completely from cloth produced in the United States.

Madison followed the usual fashion of the day and wore a coat and short pants called knee breeches. However, his choice of US-made cloth for his inauguration clothes was unusual. It was his way of trying to get people to "buy American."

According to Madison's personal slave, he always dressed completely in black.

FACT 19

Madison was an environmentalist.

After leaving the White House, Madison returned to Montpelier. He had a deep respect for and understanding of nature, including living things too small to be seen by human eyes. He warned that people might be wiped out by upsetting the balance of nature.

Madison farmed his land using methods that are today considered modern.

FACT 20

Madison was honored with his face on the US $5,000 bill.

Several Founding Fathers have their face on US coins and paper money. George Washington is on $1 bills and quarters. Thomas Jefferson is on $2 bills and nickels. Alexander Hamilton is on $10 bills. Benjamin Franklin is on $100 bills.

You've likely never seen a $5,000 bill. They're almost never used anymore.

Timeline of Madison's Life

March 16, 1751 — James Madison is born in Port Conway, Virginia.

Madison leaves Montpelier to attend the College of New Jersey. — **1769**

1776 — Madison helps Virginia form a new, independent government.

Madison attends the Second Continental Congress. — **1780**

1787 — Madison attends the Constitutional Convention and guides the framing of the Constitution.

Madison is elected to US House of Representatives and writes the Bill of Rights. — **1789**

1792 — Madison joins Jefferson in founding the Democratic-Republican Party.

Madison leaves the House of Representatives and returns to Virginia. — **1797**

1801 — Madison becomes Jefferson's secretary of state.

Madison is elected the fourth president of the United States. — **1808**

1812 — The United States goes to war against England.

British soldiers enter Washington, DC, and burn the White House, the Capitol, and the Library of Congress. — **August 1814**

December 1814 — War with England ends.

Madison ends 8 years as president and returns to Montpelier. — **1817**

June 28, 1836 — Madison dies at Montpelier.

A Great Statesman

Madison never left Virginia again once he returned to it after his years as president. He farmed his plantation. He helped Jefferson create the University of Virginia and later served as its leader. He suffered health problems in old age and spent years in bed.

But Madison remained concerned with the great issues facing his country. He worked to abolish, or end, slavery. Although he could barely bend his fingers, he wrote many letters and articles on political subjects. He has been called "our greatest **statesman**" after George Washington.

John Trumbull, who painted pictures of many of the Founding Fathers, painted this picture of Madison late in the statesman's life.

29

Glossary

college: a school after high school

constitution: the basic laws by which a country or state is governed

Constitutional Convention: a meeting that took place in 1787 to address problems in the original US constitution

Continental Congress: a meeting of colonial representatives before, during, and after the American Revolution

duel: a fight with deadly weapons between two people, with witnesses present, because of a wrong done by one to the other

environmentalist: one who supports care of the natural world

inauguration: a service marking the start of someone's term in public office

politics: the activities of the government and government officials

ratify: to give official approval to something

representative: a member of a lawmaking body who acts for voters

statesman: one who exercises leadership wisely and in the best interest of all

tyranny: government in which power is placed in a single ruler

For More Information

Books

Adler, David A., and Michael S. Adler. *A Picture Book of Dolley and James Madison.* New York, NY: Holiday House, 2009.

Dooling, Sandra. *James Madison.* New York, NY: PowerKids Press, 2013.

Gunderson, Megan M. *James Madison: 4th President of the United States.* Minneapolis, MN: ABDO Publishing, 2016.

Websites

Fun Facts on James Madison
fun-facts.org.uk/american-presidents/james-madison.htm
Discover more fun facts about James Madison on this site.

James Madison
kids.laws.com/james-madison
Find a short biography of James Madison along with more interesting information here.

James Madison
mountvernon.org/digital-encyclopedia/article/james-madison/
Read about Madison's friendship with George Washington, and watch a video of a historian talking about Madison and Alexander Hamilton.

Index